AGAINST
the TIDE

Other Books by John L. A[

*10 Things Pope Francis
Wants You to Know*

*10 Things Pope Benedict
Wants You To Know*

Global Good News

About the Author

John L. Allen, Jr., established the Rome office of the *National Catholic Reporter* in 2000 and continues to break the leading stories of the Vatican. Allen is associate editor at *The Boston Globe,* covering up-to-date Catholic news. Additionally, Allen is also the senior Vatican analyst for CNN and author of several best-selling books, including *10 Things Pope Francis Wants You to Know* and *10 Things Pope Benedict Wants You to Know* from Liguori Publications. You can follow him on Twitter: @JohnLAllenJr.

AGAINST the TIDE

The Radical Leadership of Pope Francis

John L. Allen, Jr.

Liguori
ONE LIGUORI DRIVE
LIGUORI MO 63057-9999

Imprimi Potest:
Harry Grile, CSsR, Provincial
Denver Province, The Redemptorists

Published by Liguori Publications
Liguori, Missouri 63057

To order, call 800-325-9521
www.liguori.org

p ISBN: 978-0-7648-2516-3
e ISBN: 978-0-7648-6960-0

Liguori Publications, a nonprofit corporation,
is an apostolate of The Redemptorists. To learn more about
The Redemptorists, visit Redemptorists.com.

Printed in the United States of America
18 17 16 15 14 / 5 4 3 2 1
First Edition

INTRODUCTION

For the world's news media, Pope Francis is a godsend in every sense save one: It's almost impossible to keep pace with the man. Reporters and pundits barely have time to digest one remarkable statement, gesture, or decision before he's launched five or six more.

Despite having been elected to the office in March 2013 at age 76 (he turned 77 on December 17), Jorge Mario Bergoglio has proven himself to be an "Energizer Bunny" of a pope. Quite honestly, Francis doesn't seem to have an "off" switch.

As a result, by the time this short reflection on his first year appears, there probably will have been a slew of other developments that add new details to the picture. In truth, almost everything written about Francis is out of date before it hits the bookshelves or the newsstands, and in some cases before the writer can even press the "send" button!

Yet no matter what happens from here on out, these last twelve months have left an indelible impression and brought lasting features of Francis' vision into view. Consider, for instance, six images of Francis in action that have already achieved iconic status:

- In November 2013, Francis embraced Vinicio Riva, an Italian whose face and body are terribly scarred by a genetic disorder and who says people normally go out of their way to avoid him. Riva later said the encounter helped restore his faith.

- In June, Francis invited a seventeen-year-old boy with Down syndrome named Alberto di Tullio to join him for a ride in the Popemobile. The moment left both Alberto and his father in tears.

- During Holy Week in March, Francis visited Rome's Casa del Marmo incarceration center for juvenile offenders, washing the feet of twelve inmates during a Holy Thursday service. In a break with tradition, two of the inmates he served were Muslims and two were women.

- In August, Francis met with a group of youngsters from two Italian dioceses and posed for a picture with several of them afterward, a shot taken by one of youngsters with a cell phone held at arm's length. It quickly went viral as the first papal "selfie."

- In October, another shot of Francis became a global sensation when a little boy wandered onstage during a Vatican ceremony and clung to the pope when officials tried to gently steer him away. Francis embraced the boy and took his presence in stride, at one point reaching down to pat him on the head while he continued to deliver his talk.

- In December, Francis welcomed three homeless men and their dog—named Marley, for reggae icon Bob Marley—into the Vatican to share his birthday breakfast.

If Francis is the "Pope of Mercy"—meaning a pontiff who believes that communicating God's tenderness and endless capacity to forgive and love are especially important today—then these pictures represent a sort of visual encyclical on the theme.

Francis also has taken the world by storm with his words. Aboard the papal plane returning from a trip to Brazil in July, he offered a description of his attitude toward homosexuals: "Who am I to judge?" It became the most-quoted line uttered by any public figure in 2013. Other signature phrases also became instant classics, such as his comparison in November of the Catholic Church to a "field hospital" in which the wounds of humanity are treated.

In various ways over the past year, Francis has outlined a new mission statement for the Church. Here's how he states it in his November 2013 apostolic exhortation *Evangelii Gaudium* (The Joy of the Gospel): "I prefer a church which is bruised, hurting and dirty because it has been out on the streets, rather than a church which is unhealthy from being confined and from clinging to its own security."

At the substantive level, Francis has taken a number of important reform steps during his first year, including naming a council of eight cardinals from around the world to act as his key advisors, issuing new laws on Vatican finances to promote greater accountability and transparency, creating a new commission to foster the protection of children and vulnerable adults from sexual abuse, overhauling the procedures for the Synod of Bishops to make it more participatory, shaking up the membership of the Vatican department that picks bishops, and trimming the tug of careerism in the Church by restricting the use of the title "monsignor" to priests over age sixty-five.

People around the world have been deeply charmed, and Catholics in particular sense a new wind blowing in the Church they love. As more than one commentator has observed, in the Francis era, it's "cool to be Catholic" again.

By any standard, it's been a remarkable twelve months. Since this is a pope with no down time, we probably haven't seen anything yet!

I

A MAGICAL DEBUT

From the moment Pope Benedict XVI made his stunning resignation announcement on February 11, 2013, setting it to take effect at 8 PM Rome time on February 28, speculation began to swirl about who might succeed him as the leader of the world's 1.2 billion Catholics. Plenty of names were mentioned, and while the Jesuit cardinal-archbishop of Buenos Aires, Argentina, was usually in the mix, he finished on the "B" or "C" lists of most handicappers—too old, they said, someone whose moment probably had come and gone eight years before, when he was the leading alternative to Benedict.

Thus when Jean-Louis Cardinal Tauran of France, the protodeacon of the College of Cardinals, stepped out onto the balcony of St. Peter's Basilica on March 13 to announce that Jorge Mario Bergoglio of Argentina had been elected, it came as a surprise—not a stunner, perhaps, but something of a long shot.

In the brief interval between that *Habemus Papam* announcement and the new pope's debut, the talk was of Bergoglio as a "Pope of Firsts": the first pope from outside Europe in nearly 1,300 years, the first pope from Latin America, the first pope from the developing world, the first Jesuit pope, and, of course, the first pope to take the name "Francis," expressing an entire program of governance in a single word by evoking images of St. Francis and his love affair with Lady Poverty.

That talk placed the bar of expectations fairly high when the new pontiff stepped out to present himself to the world, and what he delivered could well be taught in graduate communications programs as a model of effective debuts.

He began by saying, *"Buona sera,"* the Italian version of "good evening," a dash of simplicity that set the crowd roaring, and that's since become a signature Francis touch. He reminded his listeners that the duty of the conclave was to elect a pope, and he joked that the cardinals went "almost to the ends of the earth" to find one. He asked for prayers for Pope Benedict, and then he told the crowd that before he imparted the usual papal blessing, he wanted to ask them to pray for *him*. The new occupant of the world's most powerful spiritual office then got down on his knees, in silence, waiting for the people in the square and around the world to pray for him before he bestowed his blessing upon them.

It struck listeners that Francis referred to himself as a "bishop" and the "bishop of Rome" more than as the "pope," a convention that seemed to reflect a humbler conception of the papal office.

Those moments on the evening of March 13 captured the world's imagination, as did several other early moves in the days that followed.

We quickly learned, for instance, that after his election Francis didn't sit on the papal throne in the Sistine Chapel to receive the other cardinals, but remained standing. For his debut, he wore a simple white cassock with no red "mozzetta" (cape) and his own simple pectoral cross. After the conclave wrapped up, Francis spurned the chauffeur-driven papal limousine with the "SCV 1" license plate, standing for "Vatican City State," and instead hopped on a shuttle bus with the other cardinals. The day after his election, Francis made a point of going back to the Casa del Clero in Rome's Via Della Scrofa, a hotel for clergy where he had been staying before the conclave, to pack his own bag and to pay his own bill...the first time anyone had seen a pope pull a wallet out of his pocket to cover a debt.

Other details emerged, including the fact that the new pope had made phone calls to his newspaper delivery man in Buenos Aires to cancel his subscription and to his cobbler to ask that a pair of shoes that were in for repair be put in a box and shipped to Rome. Also, Francis devoted his first Sunday Mass as pope on March 17 not to a magnificent ceremony in St. Peter's Basilica, but to a simple liturgy at St. Anne's Church, the small parish church for Vatican employees, where he stood outside afterward to say hi to people like a simple country pastor.

Famously, Francis exclaimed, "There's room for 300 people here!" when given a tour of the papal apartment and decided instead to continue living in a modest room at the Casa Santa Marta, the Vatican residence where the cardinals stayed during the conclave.

All public figures are surrounded by a narrative that usually defines how they're perceived, and Francis had the great fortune of not stepping onto the public stage with a preexisting narrative. Rather, he got to create his own, and he did so brilliantly. Within forty-eight hours of election, the narrative was forged: A humble, simple "People's Pope" seemed determined to shake things up in the world's oldest Church.

While truckloads of new details have been added over the subsequent year, the storyline was all there in miniature after Francis' magical debut.

2

MAN OF
THE PEOPLE

Before one of his regular Wednesday general audiences in January, a morning event in St. Peter's Square when the pope delivers a sort of catechism lesson, Francis was chatting informally with some of the people in attendance when a nearby microphone picked up the exchange.

When an enthused Italian man gushed over how wonderful it is that the pope spends so much time with ordinary people, Francis quipped that he needs to stay connected with regular folks because otherwise, "I couldn't afford the psychiatrist's bill!" He gave a similar explanation in March 2013 of his decision to live in the Casa Santa Marta, saying in a letter to a friend named Fr. Enrique Martínez in Argentina that he needed a sort of "family" around him and didn't want the "isolation" that comes with the usual papal accommodations.

There's no doubt that this is a pope who craves the company of ordinary people and who is determined not to live in a gilded cage.

Whenever Francis arrives for a public event, whether it's in St. Peter's Square or on the road, he always begins by making a long swing through the crowd, usually on the back of an open-air jeep, waving and smiling. He makes repeated stops to greet people, sometimes old friends from Argentina he spots in the crowd, but often people he's never met who happen to catch his eye. Sometimes he accepts *mate* from them, the Argentine tea he's fond of, or jerseys from San Lorenzo, his favorite soccer team in Argentina that sported pictures of the pope on their shirts during their first match after his election. (They then beat their traditional rivals Colón de Santa Fe 1-0 and, for the record, made a comeback from eleventh place to win the national championship in December 2013.)

Francis consistently shows a special love for the poor and the ill during these events, part of his commitment to what he's called a "culture of encounter" in opposition to what he sees as the "throwaway culture" of the modern world. In many respects, reaching out to broken and forgotten people seems to be far more important to him than many of the usual items on the papal itinerary. Close observers of the Vatican were struck, for instance, when Francis delivered only a short pep talk to members of the Roman Curia in his Christmas address on December 21, a speech that's usually a sprawling "State of the Union" exercise. Yet that afternoon he spent several hours at Rome's Bambino Gesù Children's Hospital visiting sick children and their families. The pope stayed almost three hours at the hospital, devoting more time to that stop than to any other activity on his calendar during the Christmas season.

Even when Francis can't reach out to ordinary people in person, he's found another way to do it—by telephone. He's earned a reputation as the "Cold Call" pope for calling people he's never met for a chat, often after they've written to him to share a problem or to ask for his prayers.

In August, for instance, the pope phoned Michele Ferri, the fourteen-year-old brother of a gas-station operator in Pesaro, Italy, who had been killed during a robbery. The pope told the teenager that a letter he'd written had made him cry and promised prayers for his brother and his family. Ten days later, he called Stefano Cabizza, a nineteen-year-old engineering student who lives in the Italian town of Padova and whose family attended the pope's Mass for the feast of the Assumption in Castel Gandolfo on August 15. Cabizza had brought a personal letter for the pope to the Mass and approached a cardinal to hand it to him, asking for the pope's advice about what to do with his life. In both cases, Francis reportedly insisted on using the informal Italian *tu* rather than the formal *Lei* in speaking to the youngsters. Reportedly, he jokingly asked Cabizza, "Do you think the apostles called Jesus *Lei* or 'Your Excellency?'"

In January, the pope called an Italian woman named Filomena Claps, reaching her at her husband's bedside in a hospital in the city of Potenza. He promised to say Mass the next day for her daughter, who disappeared in mysterious circumstances in 1993 and was later found dead, and whose birthday it would have been that day.

Francis' penchant for working the phone has become such a cultural phenomenon that a famed humor columnist in Italy named Beppe Severgnini actually published a set of tips for how to handle an unexpected call from the supreme pontiff in the country's leading newspaper, *Corriere della Sera*. Here's a sample: "Don't end the conversation yourself, but let the pontiff decide when to say goodbye. If your mom, your wife, or your husband starts yelling from the kitchen, 'Come on, move it, the food's ready, get off the phone!' ignore them. Then, while you're pouring the wine, say: 'The successor of Peter says hello. So, what's for dinner?'"

This appetite for staying in touch with ordinary people is a trademark of Pope Francis' personality, but it's also an instrument of governance. One of his former priests in Argentina, Fr. Juan Isasmendi, says the big problem with Bergoglio as a boss was that "you could never lie to him" because "he knew everything."

"He'd call you to ask how things were going in the parish," Isasmendi said in an April 2013 interview, "and if you tried to feed him a line of bull, saying, 'Everything's great, no problems at all,' he'd stop you in your tracks and ask, 'What about the 400 *pesos* that went missing from the collection plate last week?'" Because he talks to everybody, Isasmendi said, he knows way more about what's happening than you might think.

One way this man has always stayed on top of details like that is by talking to everybody. This "Pope of the People," in other words, not only loves company as a person, he also benefits from it as a CEO.

3

LEADERSHIP IN SERVICE

To some extent, the gestures of simplicity that have caused the world to fall in love with Pope Francis simply arise from who the man really is. For the fifteen years he served as the Archbishop of Buenos Aires (1998 to 2013), he declined the archbishop's palace for a modest apartment so Spartan that he often had to leave the oven on 24/7 during the winter because the building couldn't afford central heat.

Thus when Elton John told *Vanity Fair* magazine in June that Francis comes off as "a miracle of humility in an era of vanity," he was definitely on to something.

Yet it would be misleading to style Francis as a naïf who bumbled into high places. He is a politically astute manager who has been in leadership in the Catholic Church all of his adult life, since he became Provincial Superior of the Jesuit order in Argentina at age thirty-six.

The lifestyle choices he's making as pope aren't simply a reflection of his personality, but they're also intended to set a new standard for leadership in the Catholic Church. In effect, what Francis seems to want is that when people look at the symbols of office in the Church, such as Roman collars and the pectoral crosses that bishops wear, they think automatically not of power and privilege but of service.

That's more than a journalistic hypothesis, because Francis has made this point out loud. In a speech he delivered to all the nuncios (papal ambassadors) of the world in June, he laid out a vision of the kind of bishop he wants them to find. What we don't need, he said that day, are bishops who have "the psychology of a prince." Instead, he said, we need "pastors who carry the smell of their sheep," because they're close to the ordinary people they're called to serve.

The heart of the pope's brief Christmas talk to the Roman Curia was likewise a warning that without a lively spirit of service, the structures of the Church "turn into a ponderous, bureaucratic customs house, constantly inspecting and questioning, hindering the working of the Holy Spirit and the growth of God's people."

We also know Francis is willing to take action to make his vision stick, a point that became clear from his intervention in the German Diocese of Limburg in October. Bishop Franz-Peter Tebartz-van Elst had become infamous as the "bling bishop" for spending roughly $42 million to remodel the bishop's residence, including more than $1 million on landscaping and even $20,000 for a bathtub. Francis dispatched a senior Vatican investigator in September and then called the bishop to Rome in October, telling him he would take an unspecified sabbatical outside the diocese while a new administration was appointed. Today, the leading theory is that the remodeled residence will be turned into either a soup kitchen or a center for immigrants and refugees.

Francis has made the same expectation clear in other ways. When he appointed a group of new cardinals in January 2014, for instance, he sent the new princes of the Church a letter asking them to keep their celebrations modest. One certainly can't accuse him of not taking his own advice, because when then-Archbishop Bergoglio was made a cardinal in 2001, he didn't even buy a new set of scarlet vestments. Instead, he had the robes of his rather portly predecessor, Antonio Cardinal Quarracino, taken in to fit.

"The cardinalship does not imply promotion; it is neither an honor nor a decoration; it is simply a service that requires you to broaden your gaze and open your hearts," the pope wrote to his new eminences. "Therefore I ask you, please, receive this designation with a simple and humble heart. And, while you must do so with pleasure and joy, ensure that this sentiment is far from any expression of worldliness or from any form of celebration contrary to the evangelical spirit of austerity, sobriety, and poverty."

Fundamentally, as Francis sees it, this isn't about Puritan severity or taking the pleasure out of life. Obviously, Francis is a guy who knows how to let the good times roll. Rather, it's about recalibrating people's impressions of what leadership in the Church looks like so the spirit of the Gospel shines through as clearly as possible. It's also an essential form of coherence from a pope named Francis who famously, just three days after his election, voiced his longing for a "poor Church for the poor."

Is the emphasis on a spirit of service having an effect? Well, here's one measure. In the spring of 2013, a veteran cardinal walked into a Roman restaurant not wearing his usual ecclesiastical finery, full of crimson and gold, but only a modest black clergyman outfit. When someone noted the change, the cardinal delivered an epigrammatic reply.

"Under this pope," he declared, "simple is the new chic!"

4
THE SOCIAL GOSPEL

Pope Francis has said and done many remarkable things that leave themselves open to divergent, and sometimes contradictory, interpretations. In fact, there are so many competing theories about the nature of the "Francis revolution" that at times he almost seems a Rorschach-style inkblot, so that people's readings of him often say more about themselves than about the pope.

One such confusion has been Francis' attitude toward Church teachings on controversial life issues such as abortion, contraception, and gay marriage. On different occasions, beginning with his airborne press conference aboard the papal plane coming back from his trip to Brazil in July, Francis has said he doesn't intend to talk a great deal about those matters because "the Church has already expressed herself perfectly." In some quarters, that was taken to mean the pope was softening or watering down the Church's pro-life stance.

By now, it should be clear that's not the case. Among other things, in his annual speech to diplomats in January, Francis referred to abortion as "horrific." Make no mistake, this is a robustly pro-life pope!

That said, it's also clear that Francis wants to lift up other elements in Catholic social teaching that he believes have not always gotten the same attention, but which he regards as equally intrinsic to the defense of human life and dignity, beginning with concern for the poor. These matters are often referred to as constituting the Church's "Social Gospel," and they are the heart of Francis' political and diplomatic agenda.

The three highest-profile and gutsiest political interventions by this pope over his first year were all based on a pillar of the Social Gospel.

On July 8, Francis made his first trip outside Rome to the southern Mediterranean island of Lampedusa, a major point of arrival for impoverished migrants and refugees from Africa and the Middle East seeking to enter Europe. Usually subjected to appalling exploitation and abuse along the way, these migrants then try to cross the sea in rickety and overcrowded boats. Some 20,000 people have died that way over the last two decades, and Francis laid a wreath in the sea on July 8 to commemorate them. He then blasted what he called the "globalization of indifference" to migrants, styling them as primary victims of a "throwaway culture." The visit proved prophetic. Two weeks later, another boatload of migrants from Eritrea, Somalia, and Ghana capsized and caught fire. Some 360 people died.

On July 25, Francis visited a notorious slum, called a *favela*, in Rio de Janeiro called Varginha, located in a small neighborhood known as Manguinhos, to tell the poorest of the poor that "the Church is with you." The pope delivered an unusually pointed rebuke to his hosts in the Brazilian government about their strategy of "pacifying" the *favelas* in an attempt to uproot organized crime and narco-traffickers. The *favela* Francis visited is known as Rio's "Gaza Strip" due to bloody clashes between gangs and the police. In 2012, security services unleashed a massive offensive, and the city boasts that today peace has returned. Francis clearly rejected that claim: "No amount of 'peace-building' will be able to last, nor will harmony and happiness be attained in a society that ignores, pushes to the margins, or excludes a part of itself," the pope said. "A society of that kind simply impoverishes itself, it loses something essential."

On September 7, Francis asked all 1.2 billion Catholics in the world to join in a day of prayer and fasting for peace in Syria, personally presiding over a four-hour penitential service in St. Peter's Square. In context, the gesture was clearly understood to express opposition to plans then taking shape in Washington, Paris, and other Western capitals to launch military strikes against the regime of Syrian President Bashar al-Assad. The Vatican under Francis unleashed a full-court diplomatic press against that idea, including summoning all the ambassadors accredited to the Holy See for a special briefing to lay out the case against using force. While it's always tough to assign responsibility for something that doesn't happen, many secular policy analysts believe Francis' strong moral stance played some role in slowing the rush to war. Nor has the Vatican let up. In January, the Vatican organized an extraordinary daylong peace conference in Rome ahead of the "Geneva II" summit, bringing together leading figures such as

American economist Jeffrey Sachs and Egyptian statesman Mohamed ElBaradei.

To summarize, Francis' three most consequential political stands during his first year were a pro-immigrant gesture, a statement of solidarity with the poor, and a clear stand against war. That's the Social Gospel in action.

Francis' rhetoric about the economy certainly has contributed to his profile as a pope of the Social Gospel. In his November apostolic exhortation *Evangelii Gaudium*, he blasted an "economy of exclusion and inequality" and called unfettered capitalism "a new tyranny," prompting American pundit Rush Limbaugh to describe the pontiff as a "Marxist." (The pope's polite reply in a December interview with the Italian paper *La Stampa* was to say that Limbaugh was mistaken, but that "I have met many Marxists in my life who are good people, so I don't feel offended.")

The Social Gospel seems destined to remain a hallmark of Francis' papacy going forward. In January 2014, for instance, we learned that Francis is preparing an encyclical letter on the environment.

That scoop, by the way, came out of a January 24 meeting between Francis and French

President François Hollande. When the media wanted to talk about the soap opera surrounding Hollande's private life, Francis wanted to talk peace and justice.

5

POPE OF MERCY

Over his first year, there were several stabs at inventing a sound bite to capture what Francis represents: the "Pope of Firsts," the "Pope of the Slums," the "People's Pope" and so on. All capture something essential, but in the long run probably the single best phrase to get to the heart of what Francis is about would be the "Pope of Mercy."

Mercy is the spiritual cornerstone of Francis' worldview, and there's a sense in which his entire program as pope can be read as an effort to lift up mercy as the most important Christian message of this time.

Each recent pope has had a catchphrase that represents his core emphasis. For John Paul II, it was "be not afraid," a call to revive the Church's missionary swagger after a period of introspection and self-doubt. For Benedict, it was "reason and faith," the argument that religion shorn of self-critical reflection becomes extremism while human reason without the orientation of ultimate truths becomes skepticism and nihilism.

For Francis, his signature idea is mercy, so much so that it's quite literally his motto. The line on his coat of arms is *miserando atque eligendo,* which comes from a homily by the Venerable Bede and means "choosing by having mercy." It's a reflection on the Gospel scene of Jesus and Zacchaeus, the tax collector, where Jesus invites Zacchaeus to follow him despite the fact that everyone regards him as a sinner.

Of all the catchphrases Francis has popularized since his election, none is more familiar than his mantra, "The Lord never tires of forgiving...it's us who get tired of asking for forgiveness." Francis has uttered some version of that line so often it probably ought to be printed on T-shirts and bumper stickers!

His emphasis on mercy was prominent in his first Sunday Mass as pope, at the Vatican's St. Anne Church, when he said, "In my opinion, the strongest message of the Lord is mercy." His emphasis on mercy was also there in the press conference on the papal plane, when Francis took a question about the possibility of admitting divorced and remarried Catholics to the sacraments. He gave an answer, saying basically that it's under consideration, and then he went on to make a broader point. In his view, he said, the present time is a *kairos* for mercy, using a Greek New Testament term that means a "privileged moment ordained by God."

"This change of epoch," he said, "also because of many problems of the Church—such as the example of some priests who aren't good, also the problems of corruption in the Church—and also the problem of clericalism, for example, has left many wounds, many wounds. The Church is a mother: It must reach out to heal the wounds, yes? With mercy. If the Lord never tires of forgiving, we don't have any other path than this one: before anything else, curing the wounds, yes? It's a mother, the Church, and it must go down this path of mercy. It must find mercy for everyone."

He made the same point to the bishops of Brazil in a speech during the trip: "Without mercy we have little chance nowadays of becoming part of a world of wounded persons in need of understanding, forgiveness, love," Francis said.

Francis' commitment to mercy is also reflected in his zeal for the sacrament of confession. When he made his first visit as bishop of Rome to a Roman parish on May 26, he got there early and told Fr. Benoni Ambarus, the pastor, that in addition to saying Mass and meeting the parishioners he also wanted to hear some confessions. That wasn't part of the program, so a startled Ambarus grabbed eight people more or less at random and lined them up outside the confessional. In part, that was Francis just trying to be a good local bishop, but in part he also wanted people to see the pope making time to celebrate the Church's premier rite of mercy.

(By the way, Roman pastors have "gotten the memo," and they always put a few confessions on the pope's itinerary when he drops by.)

Given the way mercy runs like a scarlet thread through the words and deeds of the new pontiff, one could analyze everything he's doing—from the nitty-gritty details of reorganizing the Vatican bank up to loftier matters such as the policy on liturgy and the sacraments—as an effort to ensure that when the world looks at the Catholic Church, what it sees is a community of mercy: a community that doesn't pay lip service to mercy, but one that actually practices mercy in its internal life.

To be clear, Francis is well aware that as a minister of the Christian Gospel, he's obligated to pronounce both God's mercy and God's judgment on a fallen world. Both are essential pieces of the picture, and offering one without the other would falsify the Christian message. Francis' calculation, however, seems to be that the world has heard the Church's judgment with crystal clarity, and now it's time for the world to hear—and to see, and to taste—its mercy.

6
A CULTURAL ICON

Perhaps one can debate the exact nature of the kind of reform Pope Francis intends to launch in the Catholic Church, or the precise meaning of some his signature phrases, but it's an empirical fact beyond any reasonable doubt that in twelve short months he has become a cultural icon and a media sensation.

Certainly the cardinals who elected Francis to the papacy have noticed. In July 2013, a reporter asked Timothy Cardinal Dolan of New York if Francis had turned out to be what the cardinals expected or if he was a surprise. Dolan's answer was that the cardinals knew they were electing a good manager and a man of the poor, but "we didn't know we were electing a rock star!"

Let's start with the fact that in every corner of the world where public opinion can be scientifically measured, Francis has the kind of approval ratings that politicians and celebrities would crawl across hot coals or sacrifice their children to pagan gods to obtain. A December 2013 CNN poll, for instance, found that 88 percent of American Catholics give the new pope a thumbs-up. Given the notoriously fractious state of the Catholic Church in America, where, under normal circumstances, it would be difficult to get 88 percent of American Catholics to agree on what day of the week it is, such a result is nothing short of remarkable.

Indeed, if Jorge Mario Bergoglio ever becomes a candidate for sainthood, his ability to unify the chronically divided Catholic Church in the United States might well be considered a contender for his first miracle.

When Russian President Vladimir Putin called on Francis in the Vatican in November 2013, he was asked about a *Forbes* magazine rundown that had him as the world's most powerful person, ahead of U.S. President Barack Obama, Chinese Premier Xi Jinping, and Pope Francis in fourth place. A flummoxed Putin replied, "How could anybody be more popular than this pope?"

It was a good question, given that there's hardly a newsmagazine on earth that didn't declare Francis its "Person of the Year" for 2013. The first to pull the trigger was the Italian edition of *Vanity Fair*, all the way back in June, with *Time* perhaps the most prominent journal to join the party in December. Even the pro-gay magazine *The Advocate* got in on the act, naming Francis "Person of the Year" and running a cover shot of the pope with a "No H8" sticker digitally "placed" on his face. In a somewhat similar vein, *Esquire* named Francis its "best-dressed man" of 2013 for his preference for humbler vestments, arguing that the pope had tapped into the post-modern taste for simplicity in sartorial fashion.

In January 2014, Francis also made the cover of *Rolling Stone* magazine during the same period that a graffiti image depicting the pope as a superhero spray-painted by a tagger onto a Roman wall became an overnight sensation. That tagger, Mauro Pallotta, said he was moved to depict Francis because "this pope is very pop."

The amount of media interest surrounding Francis is astronomic, so much so that even routine papal activity has been redefined as "news." When Pope Benedict XVI, for instance, visited Roman parishes, it was back-page news even in Italy; with Francis, it's the stuff of headlines all over world. When Benedict issued an apostolic exhortation, a literary genre used by the Vatican to collect the results of a Synod of Bishops, it was of interest only to specialists; when Francis published *Evangelii Gaudium* in November, summarizing a synod on evangelization, it was touted by media outlets around the world as a dramatic manifesto for change.

A study by the Catholic media network Aleteia in January 2014 found that for calendar year 2013, Francis was the most-mentioned world leader on the internet, with some forty-nine million references, and the highest average volume of searches per month on Google, with 1.74 million. Those totals put him ahead of Obama and Putin...though, it has to be said, still behind Justin Bieber.

In part, Francis has fed the media circus by making himself available. During the first year of his pontificate, he agreed to four major sit-downs with the press, all of them blockbusters. They include his airborne press conference of one hour and twenty minutes on the plane coming back from Brazil, a September interview with sixteen Jesuit publications picked up in the United States by *America* magazine, an October conversation with a leftist nonbelieving

Italian journalist named Eugenio Scalfari, and a December interview with the Italian paper *La Stampa*. Given that Jorge Mario Bergoglio only gave five extended interviews during his fifteen years as the Archbishop of Buenos Aires, it's obvious that as pope, Francis believes opening up to the media comes with the job.

In some Catholic circles, the popularity Francis presently enjoys is sometimes a source of heartburn, with bloggers and others complaining that it's based on inaccurate caricatures of the pope as a progressive "revolutionary" determined to jettison traditional teaching and practice. However annoying those false impressions may sometimes be, the bottom line is that the highest priority of the Catholic Church is supposed to be the New Evangelization, an effort to induce an often jaded secular world to take a new look at the faith, and by any objective measure Francis represents the most attractive missionary calling card that Catholicism has had in quite some time.

Francis has become the new Nelson Mandela, meaning the world's leading source of moral authority. The difference in the pope's case is that he combines personal charisma with the institutional authority of leading the world's largest Christian church, with more than 1.2 billion followers in every corner of the planet. For reasons both personal and institutional, therefore, it's unlikely that Francis will yield his iconic status anytime soon.

7
FRANCIS ON THE ROAD

Francis only took one overseas trip during his first year in office, a July 22-28 outing to Rio de Janeiro in Brazil for World Youth Day, but it was a humdinger. In the end, the trip put an exclamation point on Francis' reputation as a magnet for humanity, reaching a crescendo with a Saturday youth vigil and a Sunday Mass that each brought more than three million people to Rio's famed Copacabana Beach.

That turnout, by the way, shattered the previous attendance record for an event at Copacabana that was held by the Rolling Stones!

Popes have traveled before, with John Paul II alone making more than 100 overseas trips during his almost twenty-seven-year papacy, and popes have drawn massive crowds before. What made Francis' outing unique, aside from the fact that it represented a homecoming for history's first Latin American pontiff, was the distinctive personality he unveiled and the enthusiasm he engendered along the way.

One index of the excitement that Francis touched off came on the opening day of his Brazil swing, when frenzied admirers almost hijacked his motorcade. Another came on the third day, when the pontiff traveled to the Marian shrine of Aparecida. It's an important venue for Francis not only because of his deep devotion to Mary but because it was the setting of a meeting of the Latin American bishops in 2007 where then-Cardinal Bergoglio played the lead role in drafting a document that amounts to a charter for his missionary vision of a Church that gets "out of the sacristy and into the street."

When the Popemobile arrived at the shrine, it pulled into a supposedly secure area where about forty Latin American nuns had somehow managed to position themselves. When the pope emerged, they rushed him, shrieking like teenage girls at a Justin Bieber concert. A smiling Francis took it all in, even pausing to pose for cell-phone pictures with the frenzied sisters before making his way into the basilica.

Brazilian authorities had vowed to deploy 20,000 soldiers and police to protect the pope, and theoretically it was their job to help prevent this kind of mob scene. I later pulled aside one of the Brazilian troops to ask what had happened, and his utterly blunt reply was: "Look at me...I've got ammo strapped across my chest, I'm wearing a combat helmet, and I am not going to be the guy caught on YouTube beating up a nun!"

That was the spirit of Francis' eight days in Brazil: There was an enthusiasm for the man and his message that simply blew past anyone's capacity to keep it bottled up.

Among other things, Francis exuded a calm charisma during his first overseas trip, allowing his smile, his genuine delight in meeting people, and his homespun wisdom to do the work. During a visit to a Rio slum, for instance, he said the poor are often the most generous folks, quoting a Latin American proverb: "You can always add more water to the beans."

If proof were needed of how much Francis has changed the storyline about the Catholic Church, consider that he'd been in the global spotlight in Brazil for five days by the time Friday night rolled around, and no one had even raised the Church's child sexual-abuse scandals until he did so himself. Speaking at the end of a procession recalling Jesus' carrying of the cross, Francis said Jesus is united with all who suffer, including those who "have lost their faith in the Church, or even in God, because of the lack of consistency of Christians and ministers of the Gospel."

The veiled reference was a reminder of how much the scandals have hurt the Church. Yet the fact that they didn't cloud Francis' trip, as they likely would have for a different pope, was also a lesson in how much Francis has given the Church a new lease on life.

Francis' capacity for bracing honesty also shone through his July 27 speech to the bishops of Brazil, which many observers believe to be among the most important texts of his first year in office. Francis bluntly acknowledged the reality of massive defections from Catholicism in recent decades, both to mushrooming evangelical and Pentecostal movements and to religious indifference, and he prodded the bishops to do some soul-searching. He also expressed confidence that people can be won back by a Church that meets them where they live, projects warmth, and speaks out of "the grammar of simplicity."

Francis urged the bishops to adopt an outlook of "missionary discipleship," which he said naturally leads Christians "away from the center and toward the peripheries." The pope said the Church best fosters its missionary capacities when it sees itself as a "facilitator" of faith, not its "controller." Pastoral programs, he said, too often come off as "without closeness, without tenderness, without a caress." Speaking directly to the bishops, Francis said they should "conduct" the Church's missionary and pastoral efforts without "dominating" them.

"Bishops must be pastors," he said, "close to the people, fathers and brothers, with great gentleness, patient and merciful." Though he was speaking in Brazil, his words obviously have a much broader application.

Of course, the Brazil trip ended with Francis' impromptu airborne press conference that produced his instantly famous line on homosexuals, "Who am I to judge?"

In other words, his first road show synthesized many aspects of Francis' appeal—his magnetism, his warmth, his candor, his deeply missionary sense of the Church, and his capacity to surprise.

Officials have said on background that Francis hopes to visit Philadelphia in September 2015 for the Church's World Meeting of Families, so Americans sometime soon may have a chance to experience those qualities for themselves.

8

THE JOY
OF THE GOSPEL

If "mercy" is the single best word to express Francis' sense of spiritual and pastoral priorities, "joy" may be the best candidate to sum up his own personality and the effect he tends to have on people around him. It's also a core element of his vision of what Christian life is all about, so much so that he chose to call his first major text as pontiff, an apostolic exhortation issued in November, *Evangelii Gaudium* (The Joy of the Gospel).

(Francis released an encyclical letter titled *Lumen Fidei* in June, but it was largely prepared by Benedict XVI. *Evangelii Gaudium*, on the other hand, was all Francis.)

In the abstract, one might worry that Francis' strong emphasis on simplicity and modesty could come off as a sort of Puritanical austerity, a grim insistence on duty, and self-denial. In reality, however, he's "Franciscan" to the core, meaning that poverty and letting the good times roll are not at all at odds; rather, one flows from the other.

In July, Francis told a group of seminarians that "the Church is a house of joy, not a refuge for sad people." In October, while visiting a convent of cloistered nuns in Assisi, Francis said, "I'm so disappointed when I meet nuns who are joyless, who may smile with the smile of a flight attendant but not with the smile of joy that comes from within." In June, during a homily at his regular morning Mass at the Casa Santa Marta, which has become a regular stream of papal insight, Francis warned against Christians who confuse faith with rigidity. "They think that being Christian means being in perpetual mourning," he said. "They are not Christians, they disguise themselves as Christians. They do not know what the Lord is, they do not know what the rock is, [they] do not have the freedom of Christians. To put it simply, they have no joy."

During Advent in December, Francis devoted one of his Sunday Angelus addresses to the theme of joy. "A Christian who becomes constantly sad," he said, "can in a certain way be said to be far from Christ." But precisely for that reason, he said, we must not leave them alone, but rather we must "pray for them and make them feel the warmth of the community."

Joy is a big deal for this pope. As he put it in *Evangelii Gaudium,* an ambassador for the faith "must never look like someone who's just come back from a funeral!"

Perhaps that explains why his text The Joy of the Gospel was the closest thing Francis offered over his first year to Martin Luther King's famous "I Have a Dream" speech. In effect, the 224-page document is a vision statement about the kind of community Francis wants Catholicism to be: more missionary, more merciful, and with the courage to change.

Francis opens the exhortation with a dream.

"I dream of a 'missionary option,'" Francis writes, "that is, a missionary impulse capable of transforming everything, so that the church's customs, ways of doing things, times and schedules, language and structures can be suitably channeled for the evangelization of today's world, rather than for her self-preservation." In particular, Francis calls for a Church marked by a special passion for the poor and for peace.

The theme of change permeates the document. The pope says rather than being afraid of "going astray," the Church instead should fear "remaining shut up within structures that give us a false sense of security, within rules that make us harsh judges" and "within habits which make us feel safe."

The pope's toughest language comes when he argues that solidarity with the poor and the promotion of peace are constituent elements of what it means to be a missionary church. Francis denounces a "crude and naïve trust" in the free market, saying that, left to its own devices, the market too often fosters a "throwaway culture" in which whole categories of people are seen as disposable. He rejects what he describes as an "invisible and almost virtual" economic "tyranny" and calls on the Church to oppose spreading income inequality and unemployment, as well as to advocate for stronger environmental protection and against armed conflict.

In the end, The Joy of the Gospel amounts to a forceful call for a more missionary Catholicism in the broadest sense. The alternative, Francis warns, is not pleasant.

"We do not live better when we flee, hide, refuse to share, stop giving and lock ourselves up in our own comforts," he writes. "Such a life is nothing less than slow suicide."

That's a tough line, and from anyone else it might seem awfully bleak. In Francis' recipe for Christian life, however, the bitter never seems to overwhelm the sweet.

Perhaps the most arresting image Francis has used to underline the point came from a homily at the Casa Santa Marta in May, in the context of a warning about the danger of "bottling up" Christian exuberance.

"We'll grow old and wrinkled, and our faces will no longer transmit joy but only nostalgia, a melancholy which is not healthy," the pope said. "Sometimes these melancholy Christian faces have more in common with pickled peppers than the joy of having a beautiful life."

That's the short version of Francis' take on authentic Christianity: "Don't be a pickled pepper!"

9
THE FRANCISCAN REFORM

The conclave that propelled Jorge Mario Bergoglio to the papacy in March 2013 was quite possibly the most anti-establishment papal election of the last 100 years: The cardinals who filed into the Sistine Chapel were committed to voting for change. Over and over, in public and private comments, the cardinals said during the run-up to the vote that they didn't know who would emerge as the next pontiff, but they were determined he would be a reformer.

In this case, the cardinals were not voting for a break with the teaching of Pope Benedict XVI but with business management, fueled by a perception that the Italian-dominated "old guard" in the Vatican, once seemingly well-suited to making the trains run on time, had lost its grip. They pointed, among other things, to the global cause célèbre in 2009 over the rehabilitation of a Holocaust-denying bishop, controversies involving the Vatican bank, and the surreal "Vatican leaks" affair of 2012 that ended with the arrest, conviction, and eventual pardon of the pope's former butler, Paolo Gabriele, as the mole.

In Bergoglio of Buenos Aires, the cardinals believed they had found their man: a politically savvy Jesuit who had been in leadership in the Church his entire adult life but who had never worked a day in Rome and who had a reputation for taking the reins of power firmly in his own hands.

Francis, in other words, wasn't elected just to become a media icon or to turn the world on with his smile. He was elected to do some serious housecleaning, and over his first year he's taken substantive steps in that direction.

In April, Francis created a new council of cardinals to advise him on Vatican reform and governance of the universal Church, swiftly dubbed his "G8" body. The idea, which came out of the preconclave meetings among the cardinals, was to give pastors in the trenches a more regular voice in the decisions that have to be made in Rome, and in that sense it was a gesture toward what theologians call "collegiality," meaning shared authority.

It was striking, too, that Francis chose a set of eight men all known for their strong views, their willingness to speak out, and for the fact that they don't all think alike. Clearly, the pope wasn't looking for "yes" men, and he wanted to hear a range of opinions.

Francis has made several key personnel moves in the Vatican, including appointing a new secretary of state, by tradition the Vatican's "prime minister," who's very much cut from his own cloth. He has moved out or reduced the profile of a couple of officials known for fairly hardline stances and replaced them with pastoral moderates. He'll no doubt continue along those lines, though in the fairly small world of the Vatican the pope really needs only to make a couple such moves in order for everyone else to get the message about which way the winds are blowing.

Francis has moved aggressively to address two chronic sources of headaches for the Church: money management in the Vatican, and the child sexual-abuse scandals.

In August, Francis issued a tough set of new laws about Vatican finances, among other things beefing up the powers and expanding the role of a financial watchdog unit, created under Benedict XVI, known as the Vatican's Financial Information Authority. Earlier he created two commissions to ponder financial reform, one for the Vatican bank and one for the other economic and administrative structures of the Holy See, which includes the Administration of the Patrimony of the Apostolic See (APSA), the department that manages the Vatican's investments and real estate.

Under new President Ernst von Freyberg, in October the Vatican bank made public its first-ever independently certified financial statement, a clear step in the direction of transparency. The bank also hired the U.S.-based Promontory Group to conduct a detailed examination of the bank's roughly 19,000 accounts, which led to more than a 1,000 accounts being closed and tighter monitoring of the rest.

On the sexual-abuse front, Sean Cardinal O'Malley of Boston, the lone American to sit on the pope's "G8" council, announced in December that Francis had decided to create a new papal commission to confront the sexual-abuse scandals, both by fostering "best practices" in the fight against abuse and by advising the pope on specific cases. In a February 2014 interview with *The Boston Globe,* O'Malley said the new commission could also help develop protocols for cases in which bishops and other superiors are charged with failing to apply the Church's "zero tolerance" policy as a way of promoting greater accountability. O'Malley also said he had spoken with Pope Francis personally about the abuse scandals and said, "He's certainly aware of how serious this issue is."

As 2014 opened, more reform was in the offing, including a possible reorganization and downsizing of some Vatican departments and a streamlined communications operation. October 2014 will also bring the first edition of Francis' new-look Synod of Bishops, a gathering of prelates from around the world that Francis has overhauled in an effort to make it more participatory and more meaningful. Among other things, the synod circulated a questionnaire to Catholics worldwide in advance of the meeting in an effort to give the grassroots a voice.

To be clear, Francis' reform is more about good government than doctrinal change. Francis has said a clear "no" to the idea of women priests and insisted that his views on abortion and gay marriage are those of the Church because he's a "son of the Church." While he has opened the door to a possible relaxation of rules barring divorced and remarried Catholics from the sacraments, there's no indication of more sweeping revision to teaching on marriage.

The fact that he's not really changing teaching, however, doesn't mean Francis isn't having a massive impact on practice. The cardinals wanted a reformer, and after twelve months it's safe to say they got one.

10

THE "FRANCIS EFFECT"

How can we measure the impact Francis is having as pope? It's actually a hard question to answer, even if everyone seems to have an opinion on the subject.

One measure, perhaps, would be things that haven't happened on his watch. For instance, the stream of damaging leaks out of the Vatican has all but dried up, there have been no new major missteps such as unintentionally inflammatory remarks about other religions or explaining controversial decisions only after the bomb has already gone off, and there haven't been any major personnel appointments that in retrospect seemed terribly ill-advised.

On a global level, many analysts believe that Francis' strong opposition played some part in slowing the rush to war in September 2013, when the United States and other Western powers seemed on the brink of launching military strikes in Syria to try to bring down the regime of President Bashar al-Assad. It's impossible to parcel out responsibility with any precision, but one can make a case that Francis helped spare the world another escalation of a Middle Eastern conflict.

Using another set of metrics, some ask whether Francis' popularity is translating into any discernible bump in the usual statistical measures of ecclesiastical vitality, such as Mass attendance or financial contributions. Here the evidence is mixed.

A November study by the Pew Research Center in the United States found no evidence of any increase in the percentage of Catholics attending weekly Mass in the months after Francis' election and also no spike in the percentage of Americans who identify themselves as Catholic. On the other hand, a similar study conducted at the same time in Italy found that more than half the country's pastors report an increase in attendance at Mass and the sacrament of reconciliation that they attributed to a "Francis effect," and that "hundreds of thousands" of Italians had returned to the practice of the faith because of the new pope.

No doubt it will take time to track the data from various parts of the world, and in any event matters such as how many people in a given society take part in worship or who identify themselves with a particular religion often are related to long-term historical trajectories that are beyond the control of any one person, even a pope who also happens to be the most popular person on the planet.

At the pastoral level, there does seem to be a shift in church culture in many places, even if it's tough to assess quantitatively. One can detect it even in the Vatican, where clergy who show up for papal Masses not so long ago said that if they weren't dressed according to the traditional rule book, they would be sent back to the sacristy to change before they were allowed to take their places. Today, they report, that fastidiousness is gone, and the atmosphere is much more relaxed.

In general, one might say there's a global "loosening up" afoot in Catholicism during the Francis era, a shift away from a tight focus on discipline to a philosophy of "don't sweat the small stuff."

If another measure of a leader's impact is how much energy people invest in trying to understand his agenda, even to spin it one way or the other, then Francis has probably set new world records during his first year. Not only has an entire cottage industry sprung up of attempts to explain what Francis is all about, but when's the last time somebody like Rush Limbaugh felt compelled to publicly excoriate a pope?

Beyond the various ways one might try to put the "Francis effect" under a microscope, this is one case in which the Catholic gut isn't waiting for the ecclesiastical version of the sabermetrics crowd to weigh in. Whether people are alarmed by it or delighted with it, at the grassroots there's a wide sense that something major is happening.

Perhaps the most tangible proof of this "Francis effect" is the way the new pope has utterly changed the public narrative about the Catholic Church.

Before March 13, 2013, storylines in the global media about the Church tended to focus on the child sexual-abuse crisis, crackdowns on American nuns, assorted Vatican scandals, and bruising political controversies. While those stories have not gone away, today the dominant narrative about Catholicism has become, "People's pope takes the world by storm!"

Deeper than his pop culture appeal (for instance, he has more than eleven million followers on Twitter), Francis' charisma represents a powerful missionary calling card for the Church, one that seems to be revitalizing Catholicism and offering it a new lease on life.

If that's not a revolution, one might say, it's hard to know what one would look like. And remember, we're only a year into the story. In other words, stay tuned!